W9-CTD-198

Shadows

Carolyn B. Otto

SCHOLASTIC INC.

New York   Toronto   London   Auckland   Sydney
Mexico City   New Delhi   Hong Kong   Buenos Aires

PHOTO CREDITS: Cover: Bonnie Kamin; page 1: Michael Newman/PhotoEdit; 3: David Young-Wolff/PhotoEdit; 4: Vicki Silbert/PhotoEdit; 5: David Young-Wolff/PhotoEdit; 6: David Young-Woff/PhotoEdit; 7: Michael Newman/PhotoEdit; 8: David Young-Wolff/PhotoEdit; 9: Tony Freeman/PhotoEdit; 10: Tony Freeman/PhotoEdit; 11: Bill Bachmann/PhotoEdit; 12: David Young-Wolff/PhotoEdit; 13: David Young-Wolff/PhotoEdit; 14–15: David Young-Wolff/PhotoEdit; 16: David Young-Wolff/PhotoEdit; 17: Bill Aron/PhotoEdit; 18: Bill Aron/PhotoEdit; 19: David Young-Wolff/PhotoEdit; 20: David Young-Wolff/PhotoEdit; 21: David Young-Wolff/PhotoEdit; 22: David Young-Wolff/PhotoEdit; 23: David Young-Wolff/PhotoEdit; 24, both: Tony Freeman/PhotoEdit; 25, both: Tony Freeman/PhotoEdit; 26: Michael Newman/PhotoEdit; 27: Michael Newman/PhotoEdit; 28–29: Michael Newman/PhotoEdit; 30: Michael Newman/PhotoEdit. All photographs provided by PhotoEdit of Long Beach, CA, with the help of Leslye Borden and Liz Ely.

We are grateful to Francie Alexander, reading specialist, and to Adele M. Brodkin, Ph.D., developmental pyschologist, for their contributions to the development of this series.

Our thanks also to our science consultant Marianne Dyson, who has a degree in physics and worked for NASA as a mission controller.

Book design by Barbara Balch and Kay Petronio.

Copyright © 2001 by Carolyn B. Otto.
All rights reserved. Published by Scholastic Inc.
Printed in the U.S.A.

ISBN 0-439-69324-1

4 5 6 7 8 9 10   23   12 11 10 09 08 07

When you go out on a
sunny day, your **shadow**
goes with you.

When you skip or
swing or run, your
shadow does, too.

If the sun shines in front of you, your shadow will be behind you.

If the sun shines behind
you, your shadow will be in
front of you.

Dogs and cats have
shadows. Cars and rocks
have shadows, too.

A few **clouds** in the sky
make shadows on the ground.

But, if the sky is dark and gray, it may be too cloudy to find many shadows.

What made this shadow?

There must be **light** to make shadows. The sun makes very bright light.

A toy truck!

The sun's light comes from its heat. Other hot things can make light, too.

A fire makes light. Candles make light when they burn. Stars make light.

Electricity (i-lek-**triss**-uh-tee) makes light in lightbulbs. Even a tiny flashlight bulb can make bright light.

Take a flashlight into a
dark room. It can help you
learn more about shadows.

Shine the flashlight toward
a wall. Hold your hand in
front of the light.

The light shines on
your hand. But it cannot
shine *through* your hand.

What made this shadow?

You make shadows on the wall when your hand blocks the light.

Hold a book, or a ball, or
a toy in front of the light.

A bicycle wheel!

Every shadow you see is made
by something that blocks light.

Shadows can be many **shapes.** And shadows can change shape. They can change from short to long, or long to short.

Noon

Three o'clock

Shadows can also change from fat to thin, or thin to fat.

Sometimes shadows change because of the time of day. At noon, shadows are short. In the morning, or in the afternoon, shadows are longer.

Sometimes shadows change because the light or the object moves. Shine your flashlight on your hand. Keep the flashlight in the same spot, and see what happens when you move your hand.

Hold your hand close to the wall. Your shadow will look very small.

Move your hand closer to
the light. Your shadow will
get bigger.

Your shadow grows from
small to big because you are
blocking more light.

Bird

You can make pictures
with shadows.

24

Here are two you
may want to try.

Dog

At night, there might be
enough light for shadows, too.

Light from the windows
of a store will make shadows.

Light from a streetlight, or
the moon, can make shadows
on your walls.

Before you go to sleep
tonight, try to find all the
shadows in your room.

If you fall asleep before
you are done, that is okay.
There will be more shadows
to find tomorrow!

Glossary

clouds—tiny bits of water, snow, dust, or ice that collect in the air

electricity (i-lek-**triss**-uh-tee)—a force that can make light

light—something bright that helps you see

shadow—a dark shape made by something that blocks light

shapes—the forms of things

Have you ever seen your shadow on a bright and sunny day? Do you know what a shadow is? Are you curious about how shadows change their shapes?

Learn all about shadows in this book full of facts and photographs.

www.scholastic.com

ISBN 0-439-69324-1

9000

9 780439 693240